DATE DUE

DEMCO 38-296

FLYING BLIND

Also by the author

SALT AIR
Wesleyan University Press, 1983

OBJECTS OF AFFECTION
Wesleyan University Press, 1987

Ed. WHERE WE STAND:
WOMEN POETS ON LITERARY TRADITION
W.W. Norton & Company, 1993

FLYING BLIND

poems by

SHARON BRYAN

Sarabande Books

Library of Congress Cataloging-in-Publication Data:
Bryan, Sharon.
    Flying blind / Sharon Bryan.—1st ed.
        p.   cm.
    ISBN 0-9641151-6-6 (cloth : alk. paper).—ISBN 0-9641151-7-4
    (paper : alk. paper)
    I. title.
    PS3552.R877F59   1996
    811'.54—dc20   96-86

Cover Painting: Laura K. Popenoe
"A Soul Song," 1987

Cover and Interior Design by Tree Swenson

Manufactured in the United States of America
This book is printed on acid-free paper.

Sarabande Books is a non-profit literary organization.

Letters are symbols that turn matter into spirit.

ALPHONSE DE LAMARTINE

All I know is what the words know.

SAMUEL BECKETT

ACKNOWLEDGMENTS

Grateful acknowledgment is made to the following publications, in which some of these poems first appeared:

The Atlantic Monthly: "-Esque"
Crazyhorse: "Bonne Chance," "Synecdoche"
Denver Quarterly: "Slip of the Tongue"
The Georgia Review: "Kid Gloves," "Away," "Beholden"
The Gettysburg Review: "Ultrasound," "What Biology Is All About"
Hayden's Ferry Review: "Imitations of Mortality"
The Missouri Review: "Theory"
The Nation: "Wish You Were Here"
Network: "Beyond Recall"
Ploughshares: "Dead Air," "Indirect Objects"
Poetry Northwest: "Housing"
Quarterly West: "Weird Niece"
River Styx: "Be-"
The Seattle Review: "Conjugation," "Full of Himself," "High Heels,"
     "Minutiae," "Hopeless"
Seneca Review: "Belie"
The Southern Review: "Trimmings," "Wrappings"
Tar River Poetry: "Abracadabra," "Foreseeing," "Foretelling,"
     "Subjunctive," "Sweater Weather," "This," "Unhinged"
Weber Studies: "Frankly," "I Haven't Got All Day," "You Are Here"

I would also like to thank the National Endowment for the Arts, Memphis State University, and the Tennessee Arts Commission for grants that made time available for some of this writing.

A number of poems in this book are indebted to the arguments presented in Stephen J. Gould's *Wonderful Life* (Norton, 1990).

CONTENTS

FLYING BLIND

ABRACADABRA

A man was dying —
slowly at first, he said,
then the river he was riding

divided, he went one way
everyone else the other,
soon for him there was nothing

but darkness and pain —
he was adamant about that,
no welcoming light —

then he began to fall, it was
the feeling that yanks us back
from the edge of sleep,

but not him, not this time,
he kept on dropping
for what seemed like forever,

just the twist in the pit
of his stomach to tell him
he was still alive,

still falling, until finally
there was something
else, a little tickle

at the back of his mind,
a notion that might slow him
if only he could get hold of it —

what he needed was a word,
a particular word,
but none came to him

for another long time,
then one began to take shape —
the pain was even worse

at first, but he wasn't falling
as fast, and then at long long last
he stopped:

this was just the beginning
of coming back, he had to feel
his way up the well

he seemed to have fallen down,
lifting his entire weight
every inch with his fingertips,

it took hours or days,
he couldn't tell which — and the word
that had made it possible

was *hope* — when he came to that part
of the story, we were embarrassed,
we looked at each other and not

at him: it was too obvious, too
sentimental, a sign of weakness
in a strong man, we chalked it up

to his illness — but what did he care
about irony and narrative
distance? He knew he'd sat up

in bed, asked for his shoes,
and taken his son to a movie,
Conan the Barbarian.

He lived another year
on that one word plucked
from thin air.

for Richard Blessing

AWAY

It's an adverb, not a place
the dead could stay
or come back from,

almost an accident
of language that we say
they *go,* so have to wonder

where, when we really mean
they *stop,* as music does,
diminuendo — we weave

these tangled webs
not necessarily to deceive,
but because one word

leads to another, it's easy
to get carried away,
in no time at all

we're out on a limb
or up a creek without
a paddle — the pull

of our new toy was irresistible:
we followed it here,
then the door disappeared

behind us, as another one will
when we leave the air
for good — that is, forever —

but we would like to believe
that the living will still
receive us, even as nothing

more than a whispered phrase,
a word in your ear that seems
to come out of nowhere.

B E-

A begat B begat C
and here we are at the depot,
surrounded by more baggage

than we could ever carry
alone, begirt, a little bedraggled,
but beguiled by what lies

before behind beyond us
and the power of a prefix
to make a noun a star:

bedecked, bedizened, bejeweled,
there must be something special
under all that finery, if only

a swirl of longing we've given
a name to, and a voice — why not,
we're all born ventriloquists,

so good we feel betrayed
when the world won't speak
for itself — but nothing escapes us,

no matter how far we fling it,
and we're never entirely taken in
by *trompe l'oeil* and *trompe l'oreille*,

we're proud of our double vision,
our ability to see and see through
the illusion — it's just that

sometimes we'd like to close one eye
and believe wholeheartedly in objects
that don't depend on us

for their definition, not a world
of absence but one in which
we'd have everything to lose.

BEHOLDEN

It never stops, the feeling
of being under observation,
waving to the camera, to mom,

to god, but somewhere along the way
the possibility leaks in like light
streaking this winsome picture

that your life is not held
in anyone's mind (including
your own, a poor housekeeper

who prefers a good story
to a porridge of facts),
that it isn't even a handful

of dust but a smattering
of atoms, briefly legible
as eddies of local weather —

thus the joy beyond reason
when an old friend takes you
for the person you used to be,

or a total stranger smiles
and says Hello and wants nothing
in return but to have caught

your eye in passing.

BELIE

Why not believe our eyes
when they say the sun rises
and sets, instead of gossiping
about what goes on behind

the world's closed doors,
telling one wild story after
another: gravity, DNA, the id?
Maybe the story's the heart

of the matter, what we make
of having awakened in the dark,
a few faint sounds and flashes
of light to go on, and an urge

to explain ourselves, to invent
more means of travel than
the wheel: *and then . . . and then . . .*
for all its flash and charm,

sight doesn't have an inside track
on reality, it's just one
more way to look at things,
or two more ways, an inch

apart, like almost matched
accounts by twins of why
they're late getting home —
the discrepancies give us

a measure of what we're up against:
revelations that may conceal
nothing, or trivial truths,
or the music of the spheres,

or our starkly simple fears.

BEMUSED

An American crossing
an English street heeds
the instructions at his feet:

Look Right, but then in-
voluntarily looks left,
in response to a voice he's heard

for forty years: he *cannot*
not look, the body learns
its lessons so well — think

what it must take to make it
stop, as if it had resented
every pinprick, every command

to take another breath, hoarded
its grievances like a bitter servant
until it had more than enough

to buy its way out with one
resounding N O followed by
an infinity of zeroes.

BEYOND RECALL

Nothing matters
to the dead,
that's what's so hard

for the rest of us
to take in —
their complete indifference

to our enticements,
our attempts to get in touch —
they aren't observing us

from a discreet distance,
they aren't listening
to a word we say —

you *know* that,
but you don't believe it,
even deep in a cave

you don't believe
in total darkness,
you keep waiting

for your eyes to adjust
and reveal your hand
in front of your face —

so how long a silence
will it take to convince us
that we're the ones

who no longer exist,
as far as X is concerned,
and Y, that they've forgotten

every little thing
they knew about us,
what we told them

and what we didn't
have to, even our names
mean nothing to them

now — our throats ache
with all we might have said
the next time we saw them.

BONNE CHANCE

From our point of view,
the longest day of the year,
the sun seems to hover on the horizon.
The universe didn't have us in mind,

but what would it all mean
if we hadn't stumbled on the scene,
eager to explain our accidental
existence? No mouthpiece, no story.

And no distinguishing good from bad
luck: everything might have been
otherwise. Life might have stayed
in the sea, tonight's dinner

been overcooked, we might have had
our backs to the window,
missed the cat batting a butterfly,
the children who have stopped their game

to watch — their words more poignant
because we can't hear them.
It might have been raining.
The little flecks on the x-ray

might have been a malign constellation.
We might not have had a future
tense, or subjunctive, language thicker
with what isn't than what is.

CONJUGATION

One announcer uses the word *vaporized,*
describing what probably happened
to the astronauts, and it proves

so consoling it becomes the official
version: transported from one state
to another without the gradual ravages

of travel. A blessing for the living,
who use it to presume death can be blesséd.
Thus the dismay when a foot, still clad

in a blue sock, washes up onshore.
No surprise to the nine-year-olds
who asked a classmate if he saw bodies

falling, and if he did, was there blood
on them? He hadn't seen, but he believed
the salt water would have washed everything

clean. They took that small comfort,
less than the rest of us seemed to require.
Vapor: the third stage of matter,

of conjugation — after ice and water —
as if change could be accomplished without
loss, and death were such a change

of pace, of form, the content somehow
continuing. But there is all that fact
of matter, of muscle, bone, blue nerve

to be got through, got out of the way
of whatever might rise, might be teased out
from the perishables by the right worm,

right wind and rain, right scouring blast.
A death that combines dying with undoing
is pristine: we could hope they had found a way

to take their bodies with them — *crossing
over, crossing over* — until the unmelted flesh
began to surface, form without content

yet filled with meaning: the part comes to stand,
as well as it can, for the whole —
being, conceivably, all that remains.

DEAD AIR

Better to have three announcers
trip over each other's tongues
than let silence go out

like a lethal gas over the airwaves —
as if silence were anything
but a figment of our imaginations:

when would we ever have heard it?
Even before we were born
bass thudded through the walls

all hours of the night and day,
and back before we had ears,
DNA was tapping out its message

in our cells, so silence
must be another of the gods
we've invented out of dread

and need, not just to scare
ourselves, but to prepare the way,
getting the house ready for company

that won't arrive until we're gone.

DISINGENUOUS

How many times does it turn
on itself, saying forget
what you've heard, as the judge

tells the jury to disregard
the preceding remarks?
Only once, since *genuous*

doesn't exist, except here,
where it could mean
"of the knee," as in *genuflect,*

and its opposite be *upstanding.*
As it is, in a sense: *straight-
forward, innocent, natural,*

freeborn. The naked truth,
innocence in its birthday suit.
Falsity therefore only a coverup,

not a corruption of the flesh.
The woman in bright blue
winds sinuously through

the room, dressed to tantalize.
So words intimate their truths
by averting our eyes.

DISSEMBLING

So much of the time saying No
by constructing an adjacent rococo Yes,
a sort of heroic simile that will carry

inquisitors away from the facts:
the pearl disguises a minor irritation,
birds give us a song and dance

away from their nests. So is art
the art of denial? The better the magician,
the less we trust our own senses,

yet the more their workings are affirmed:
no flight without gravity.
Let me tell you a story:

I'm going to saw this woman in half.
All good stories are true
to the grain, true blue, beautiful.

Hyperbole — like the pearl. Gainsaying
rather than denial. Let's keep an eye
on what's impossible, its friction

with what is. If we should fall
for the warm caress of our own rhetoric,
a real woman's real blood will spatter

the stage. And we need her as constant reminder
of all that we point away from
when we unfurl our impractical jokes.

-ESQUE

As wonderfully ornate and un-
necessary as a handlebar
moustache, or a handkerchief

just so in an old man's
breast pocket, not an empty
decoration but a ruffle

and flourish, a flair
for the dramatic, blesséd
excess — like the white-haired

gentleman who has shined his shoes
and put on a coat and tie
to buy groceries —

and like the intricate
orthography that spells out
our history with such pomp

and circumstance, reveals
the most delicate and indelicate
details of where we've been —

silent letters are as crucial as air
in a soufflé: imagine a ballet
dancer caught flat-footed

in an *arabesk,* or the jokes
like lead balloons if the show
were only *burlesk* — the echoes

we hear in *grotesque,*
the ancient caves we painted
our way out of,

are the voices of those
so eager for us to hear
what they had to say

they invented the alphabet
to carry their words light-
years into the heavens, here.

FLYING BLIND

We can't quite see
the world, but we have it
in translation, we say it

in words we learn to live on,
live by, as we fly high
and low, the cockpit dark,

only the glowing dials
to tell us where we are
in relation to this or that

landmark or loved one
or far-off star — and as we rush
through the turbulent air

that will eventually
engulf us, we hum to ourselves
to keep ourselves on course,

to keep our courage up,
to serenade the universe
that refuses to meet our eyes.

FORESEEING

Middle age refers more
to landscape than to time:
it's as if you'd reached

the top of a hill
and could see all the way
to the end of your life,

so you know without a doubt
that it has an end —
not that it *will* have,

but that it *does* have,
if only in outline —
so for the first time

you can see your life whole,
beginning and end not far
from where you stand,

the horizon in the distance —
the view makes you weep,
but it also has the beauty

of symmetry, like the earth
seen from space: you can't help
but admire it from afar,

especially now, while it's simple
to re-enter whenever you choose,
lying down in your life,

waking up to it
just as you always have —
except that the details resonate

by virtue of being contained,
as your own words
coming back to you

define the landscape,
remind you that it won't go on
like this forever.

FORETELLING

Once it was the gods
who tested a hero's mettle
by showing him the shape

of his own death
but giving him no way
to change things,

so that the only variable
was how he carried himself
into a future he already knew

by heart — he wasn't fighting
for his life, but to be remembered
for his manner of dying,

how he made the inevitable
his own — now doctors
interpret the omens and say

what the future holds,
delivering the news
as dispassionately as possible,

and those who receive it
are ordinary citizens
whose bodies have become

battlefields — they can't simply
withdraw to their tents and wait
for things to blow over,

can't flee the flames —
those who become heroes
find a way to go forward

without hope to propel them,
but also without despair,
as if they had entered

another dimension, a state
of grace, maybe, except
that it isn't conferred

but requires a continuous act
of will and concentration —
though they didn't choose it,

they step into the part
as if they'd been born to it,
as if the spirit spoke —

however reluctantly —
in unforgettable accents
what the body had written.

FRANKLY

I have some bad news.
Or maybe good news, depending
on how you feel, what you want —
not as in lack, of course,

but as in what you desire,
long for, hope for, would be
miserable in the absence of.
Perhaps I overstate. Let me

back up. I have some news.
Not that you don't already know
how I feel, about some things
at least, but inexactly,

and I'm about to say exactly
what I mean, as much as that's
ever possible, to strip away
confusion with the deft hands

of my words. Or to slip
the shapeless swirl of imminent
meaning into its proper nouns,
the sleeves of its blue blazer.

Whether words dress or undress,
they're smeared with the world's dirt —
and who would have it otherwise,
make language the crisp nametags

at a convention of things?
Look how far this effusion
has brought us, how far it will carry
in every indirection, giving and taking

shape in the mind's deepest trenches,
more paradoxical than the blind
neon fish I could bring up now
to illustrate the simpler mystery

of anything that remains unspoken.

FULL OF HIMSELF

And why not, it's not
for long, soon we'll all be
empty of the fluids it takes

to keep our spirits up, their nectar
replaced by chemicals incompatible
with life as we knew it

that preserve our bodies
for future generations
of archaeologists — or if you ask

that your hollow leg be fed
to the fire, just that residue
of ash will be left behind —

out of which a sprig of green
might spring, if only someone
had the temerity to water it —

not as a ballad vine
twines out of a lover's heart,
but as a volunteer appears

nonchalantly amid the ruins.

HIGH HEELS

They can dent cement,
they concentrate so much height and history
here and there, here and there.
We could learn to infer circumstance

from their half-moon inscriptions:
an angry woman, a woman of means.
A woman hurrying to her lover,
a woman pondering a passage from Kant.

Just shinny up the rope
from effect to cause, from imprint
to avoirdupois. But words
are a different matter, leave us

midair, no way to see out
of this valley of arbitrary signs —
just one billboard after another
between us and what we think of

as the tawdry, voluptuous world.
Yet whatever they overlook,
those signs are the only windows,
sight and insight, dappled glass.

Sharp enough to pierce the heart,
impractical as the spindly shoes
in which we sashay through our days,
and never our feet on the ground.

HOPELESS

If there's no chance
of getting what you want,
you can restore hope

by asking for less: if not
long life, a few years.
A few months, weeks, days.

A sweet pine box.
In this way you can go on
finding things to be grateful for —

not without a certain amount
of bitter irony, but this too
is an answer to your prayers:

let me not whine,
let me not ask Why me,
let me not outlive

my sense of humor —
the surest saving grace —
let hearing remain,

so that music and words
are the last attachments
to fail — just see

how the list grows:
even the smallest hope
wants something —

what a luxury
to be able to say *Oh honey,*
you're hopeless,

without giving it
a second thought,
just sitting on the porch

on a summer night,
laughing and talking,
nothing special unless

you see it slipping
through your fingers,
see your own absence

eavesdropping at the edge
of the lawn, waiting patiently
for you to join it.

for Matthew Hansen and Ripley Hugo

HOUSING

Animal, vegetable, mineral, kingdom
of heaven, once the architect begins
to sketch the walls, rooms rise
before your eyes, lights go on,

darkness gathers in the corners,
there's a place for everything:
bats in the belfry, aspidistra
in the parlor, tomatoes ripening

in the fruitbowl — arrangements
so compelling it's easy to forget
they're hypothetical enclosures,
disclosures, we're so quick to relax

in front of the imaginary fire,
stare out the picture window —
you can dynamite brick to dust,
but what does it take to remodel

the mind's beloved structures,
the obtuse angles that persist
long after you've gone from room
to room extinguishing the lights?

I HAVEN'T GOT ALL DAY

You'd think we'd be afraid
that saying would make it so
too soon — maybe it's shorthand:

not that I am, but if I were
about to die, I'd rather be otherwise
engaged, in the embrace

of some warm-blooded beloved,
listening to Glenn Gould hum along
with Bach's interlocked measures

of time slipping through our fingers,
the fugue figuring our losses,
our desperate wish that the voices

persist — but one by one they fall
silent, go inside or outside,
depending on your perspective —

so what to make of the moments
when one who's long gone
whispers right in your ear,

as if a phrase replayed
long after the record
was back in its jacket?

As if some sounds
had an afterlife
like light from extinguished stars.

IMITATIONS OF
MORTALITY

Why would we teach our dogs
to play dead, except to revive them
by snapping our fingers —

as if we could bring death indoors,
like a pet or a houseplant
or a bad dream exposed

to the light of day —
it begins to seem like
one of the family, asleep

at our feet in all the photos,
and we're so proud of ourselves
for having learned to live with it

we come to think it speaks
our language, understands
our heartfelt words: *good dog,*

bad dog, not yet, when all it heeds
is the high-pitched whine
of the body calling it home.

INDIRECT OBJECTS

You'd think we'd be used to it,
but it's an odd party,
all of us in one room

the world in the other,
language in its white gloves
circulating with finger foods

and billets-doux — for you?
For you? What to do
but take its word for things

— our humble servant, our only
foreign correspondent,
making some kind of sense

of the bangs and murmurs we hear
through the wall — we're so grateful
for any news, we don't insist

that the stories be consistent,
we seem to forget we're the very ones
who put the words in our mouths.

KID GLOVES

We go through life with our hands out,
taking, taking: *reception, perception,*
conception, exception, all variations
on *take hold of, to seize* . . .

our words reveal our greed —
unless the weight falls
on taking to heart
rather than taking from:

let the preposition inflect
your elbow, for taking up,
taking in, taking hold,
lest you misapprehend,

hurrying after a burrowing clam,
how near the surface
it hopes to hide,
how much for show its shell,

until you feel the flesh shrink
too late, fatally exposed,
from your blunt touch —
it must have been a moment

of surpassing hope and kindness
when humans first looked into
their own hearts and minds
and invented words to keep the world

just out of reach.

LODGINGS

Here we are, living above our bodies
like eccentric aunts in the attic,
eavesdropping on all the commotion

downstairs. Some news seems to travel
the spine's grapevine unaccompanied:
our hands know nettles from petals

without the names. But if language
is a membrane like the lung,
filtering our ex- and inspirations,

then every cell reeks of it, stinks,
is tainted, tinctured, matter instinct
with mind, mind indistinct

from matter. No lungs, no breath.
No words, no flesh — at least not
so we'd know it. No slumming,

no heading downtown unaccoutered
by the family jewels, no swimming
upstream without language

on our backs, no getting out
of our element: future, past,
absence, rapping on the walls

for a hollow spot, our knuckles
saying *not not not.* Even so
we keep trying to peek behind

the scenery we've spent forever
nailing together: Main Street,
the bank, the saloon —

the facade's the thing:
the louvered doors open
on infinite impossibilities.

MIMNERMUS
OF SMYRNA

But we are like the leaves that flowery spring puts forth,
Quick spreading in the sun's warm light. . . .

A poet couldn't ask
for a better name, but his words
are the same old story: life is beautiful

and brief — so why have we saved
a 3,000-year-old version of it
when we have so many newer ones

to choose from? Maybe because the dead
take so much with them, any fragments
left behind remind us the past

was flesh and blood, not a figment
of our imaginations, not a dream
but lives like our own, ones we can feel

the texture of between our fingers,
now rough muslin, now the whisper
of silk — and nothing does this better

than words, the net that caught
his very voice as it rose like smoke
from his body's smoldering fire

and releases it each time we read-
hear-speak his words and feel ourselves
quicken in the dwindling light.

MINUTIAE

Having things is a way to forget
about them: straight teeth, enough
food, the midnight blue silk dress.

As if memory and longing were kissing
cousins, and to have were to quench
the light and heat of desire.

So writing things down, love
or the list of groceries, is a way
to leave them behind, perfused

with a certain day that will rise
like ether from the wrinkled page
when you come across it. Forgetting

keeps things whole by letting them
go — the woman become a tree,
for example, or the man a constellation.

What clings to us is incidental,
dust too fine to cohere
and become forgettable.

ODE TO THE *OED*

What a ridiculous idea,
thinking someone could gather
every meaning of every word

ever uttered in English —
James Murray didn't want
the job, but once he took it on

he went at it tooth and nail,
hammer and tongs, until
he was literally a man

of the letters he had loved
since he could tell, at two,
"round *o*" from "crooked *s*" —

his study began to fill
with slips of paper
citing words in their natural

habitat, words on the wing, singing
their hearts out — then
he had to arrange them

so they would tell the true story
of their travels, exactly
what they'd seen — the task

was as impossible as any
in fairy tales, his assistants
only human, he assembled

his masterpiece bit by bit
by hand, he just kept at it:
pelican and *penguin* alone,

he told a friend, were more work
than two books, he was proud
of *ketch* and *tallow*,

when a friend was dying
he offered to send him *take*
if that would lift his spirits . . .

Murray must have dreamed —
alphabetically, of course —
of finishing what he'd begun,

of setting foot on dry land
after rowing across an ocean
of words, must have wearied

of the Herculean labors,
must have stood, some mornings,
outside his study, his hand

on the knob, thinking, I can't
go on — and then he went in.
When he died he was working on *un-*.

SENTENCES

Little filaments feeling their way,
defining the world as what they can safely
entwine, pumpkin or sweet pea each true

to its own simple or complex kind,
one a quick, straightforward grasp,
the other spiraling, dangling, parsing

air, taking shape and giving shape
in equal measure, spelling in neon
green what they know of the world:

so hands light their own way over
a face, a body — wordlessly,
maybe, but following the contours

of noun, verb, direct and indirect
object, every preposition, dependent
and independent clause — and why

would we have adjectives and adverbs
unless we were meant to use them?
How beautiful? How inexpressibly.

The sentence branches like capillaries,
we follow it as far as we can
before we come to a full stop,

fall out of its good graces,
out of a common language
into our separate selves.

How capital the letter that signals
our intention to proceed with a new
exploration, divinely carnal conversation.

SLIP OF THE TONGUE

Modeled on mouth of the river, eye
of the hurricane, *plume de ma tante*,
mother of god, rather than land's end,

cat's-paw, dogsbody, even cowslip,
the ruffled guernsey. For the tongue
it's more verb than verbiage —

forthright tread on the waiting peel
and you're someplace you never meant
to be, *pacem* Freud, upended by accident

so often you'd think it the essence
of life as we know it: brief stars
from the pratfall, landscape recast

when your hat droops over your eyes —
or you're possessed by an apostrophe's
new moon in the window in honor

of some past lapse, lisp, skipped beat —
it's a bad translation that doesn't
have a few: The Last Tape of Krapp,

Do Not Be Cruel, new wrinkles
ironed into the starched curtains,
house and woods across the way

fastidiously *dérangés*—
even these recent errors better
than none to remind us

it's not the model that matters,
but where we nip and tuck the fabric,
the way it all depends.

SUBJUNCTIVE

If only it were true
that someone's death
was in the cards,

in the stars,
we wouldn't torment ourselves
going over each detail

that led up to it,
trying to change something —
it's almost unbearable

to know how small a thing,
how accidental, it takes
to seal what we call

our Fate but is simply
a row of dominoes falling,
subject to wind, the table

tilting, even defects
in manufacture — after
the fact we can calculate

cause and effect, how one
followed the other
inexorably, but the end

was *not* contained
in the beginning —
not a goddess's breath

deflecting a spear,
but chance and happenstance
enter in: X might have been

alive except for a cell's
mistake, Y if she hadn't
gone swimming, Z

if the rope hadn't frayed —
and of course the wind blows
the other way: A came out

of the coma, B stepped back
in time from the curb,
C responded to treatment,

not to providence or prayer —
no reason not to be grateful
for the daisy chain of luck

we and everything else
in the world depend on,
depend from.

SWEATER WEATHER:
A LOVE SONG TO LANGUAGE

Never better, mad as a hatter,
right as rain, might and main,
hanky-panky, hot toddy,

hoity-toity, cold shoulder,
bowled over, rolling in clover,
low blow, no soap, hope

against hope, pay the piper,
liar liar pants on fire,
high and dry, shoo-fly pie,

fiddle-faddle, fit as a fiddle,
sultan of swat, muskrat
ramble, fat and sassy,

flimflam, happy as a clam,
cat's pajamas, bee's knees,
peas in a pod, pleased as punch,

pretty as a picture, nothing much,
lift the latch, double Dutch,
helter-skelter, hurdy-gurdy,

early bird, feathered friend,
dumb cluck, buck up,
shilly-shally, willy-nilly,

roly-poly, holy moly,
loose lips sink ships,
spitting image, nip in the air,

hale and hearty, part and parcel,
upsy-daisy, lazy days,
maybe baby, up to snuff,

flibbertigibbet, honky-tonk,
spic and span, handyman,
cool as a cucumber, blue moon,

high as a kite, night and noon,
love me or leave me, seventh heaven,
up and about, over and out.

SYNECDOCHE

Someone must have said,
primly, *That's your body,*
because whenever a body was found,
in a book or on the radio,

I pictured what I knew
of genitals: lemon size and shape,
lipped, hairless — or darkly furred,
like my mother's. I saw it

distinct and whole in a field
just off the road; pulled dripping
from a river; centered
on a living room rug. Charged

with intensity, like fragments
of adult conversation. Yet also
neutral — the same figure
for male or female, the same

odd fruit in any landscape.
Lost sight for years
of that useful error:
empty bodies are all alike.

Another mistake, presumably,
thinking of the body as vessel,
the spirit as escaping gas.
Maybe it's the mind that fails

to contain the body, as mine
lost faith in an image
that once held life and death
in radiant solution.

THEORY

That monocle in the middle,
the silent O, gives you something
to look into and out of,

a windowsill to rest your elbows on
while you watch the parade —
you can feel the drum's vibrations

all the way up here, the tremor
in the flag-bearer's thighs,
sweat in the trumpeter's armpits —

that's the trouble, it's all so vivid,
what's to be gained by dragging
your two left feet down there,

into the fray — even if you're hungry
for love, your eyes are always bigger
than your stomach for it, the aroma

of soup can sometimes fill you up —
your theory is full of holes, open
mouth, enlargéd eye — look out,

look out, a rowdy child
is writing with her damp finger
on the glass: O I C U R M T .

THIS

is what our arms are full of,
momentarily, what steps forward
out of the shadows to bask
in our attention, full of itself

and the present, this pain, pleasure,
weather, red-cheeked peach,
rather than that, though it's not always
chosen, some of it lands in our laps

unbidden, sometimes we can't remember
how it got there, got here, how we did,
believing in giving ourselves over
to what's in front of us, in the foreground,

under our noses: this play of light
on the water — as if there were always
other possibilities, as if any given
were defined by what it's not,

each nodding blossom reeking of how many
pinched-back buds? We happened along
willy-nilly ourselves, eager to put things
in perspective — don't let a busy background

distract from your subject, lift something
out of the muck, put a picket fence around it
to keep it in focus. Meantime the wilderness
thickens, but never mind the ripe berries

hidden in the tangle of vines.
You can't have everything, and anyway,
your hands are full: the cost
of all this is that.

TRIMMINGS

Never fished, never cleaned
a fish, so I'm stupidly surprised
by all the blood in the bag
of heads and tails. Must have thought
cold blood meant no blood
or blue blood, not this bright red
looking just like mine or anyone's
as it spatters counter, sink,
my empty white coffee cup.
Not squeamish, never was,
and used to flaying animals
in biology lab, prying
the skin loose, teasing nerves
from muscle, never asked
to put it back together.
No vegetarian, except to save
money, i.e., no scruples
about eating my dim-witted
cousins. So what rose
in my throat at the sight
of these drops, daubs, smears,
before I could rinse them away?
Oh no, I said over the fish,
involuntary prayer, apology,
thank you: you shouldn't have.
These rude parts were free, a gift.
The more elegant middle flesh
cost an arm and a leg. Almost
bare bones will still thicken soup,
still imply all they once held dear.

ULTRASOUND

Sounds too high-pitched
for even our dogs to hear
show us the body's interior,

an underworld so murky
we need an interpreter
to tell us what we see:

blocked artery, a baby's
budding arms, the beginnings
of life or death — an artificial

distinction, of course,
but one that means everything
to a given person

on a given day, who waits
for the shadowy landscape
to be put into words,

for the murmur of flesh
rearranging itself
to be translated

into human terms: hope
and fear, a story
we can briefly call our own.

UNHINGED

When is a door not a door?
When it's ajar. But in fact
that's when it's most a door,

controlling the flow of traffic
in and out with infinite
subtlety, making the mind

feel at home, not just surrounded
by weight-bearing walls,
but free to take in what it likes

of the passing parade, to linger
on the porch for last good-byes,
one hand on the doorknob,

solitude just inches away —
no wonder it's terrifying
to imagine that door ripped loose

from its pins by a violent wind
that overturns the furniture
and all our expectations —

no wonder our parents
were so intent on teaching us
to shut the door in winter,

open it in summer, the basics
of taking care of ourselves
in ordinary weather.

WEIRD NIECE

Or is it *wierd neice?*
As soon as you write it
wrong you can tell

by the way it makes you
queasy, like putting on
someone else's glasses:

the world is out there
but askew, you're aware
of what you're looking through,

a filigree of letters
that opens and discloses
a point of view, a scenic

turnout — or in this case
a wrong turn, a cul-de-sac,
a brief glimpse of possibilities

pulled back from, little
slipups, a gawky girl
almost the spitting image

of the one you meant
to write about, summoned
in error, abandoned

by the side of the road,
faint but unforgettable
in the rearview mirror.

WHAT BIOLOGY
IS ALL ABOUT

Sheep eyes, slime, dissected
frogs, you'd be amazed
how many people buy
what I sell, even women

in dainty dresses just love
to get ahold of this goo,
the afterlives of animals
much like ourselves, so

they can teach us something
about the bodies we live in,
as long as we keep in mind
they don't have minds themselves,

their eyes are just eyes,
not windows on the soul.
I don't deal in speculation,
my customers want facts —

not that bodies don't imply
a surrounding atmosphere,
but who's to say it's anything
more than natural humidity

rising from all that dampness
cells seem to thrive in —
you wouldn't call steam
floating over a lawn on a hot

summer morning a spirit,
would you? But when it comes
to people, then you've got
your cathedrals, your holy wars,

all that fuss — the best way
to think about god or anything
else is with both hands full
of this cooling flesh.

WISH YOU WERE HERE

As if the dead were just poor
correspondents on vacation,
we invent their messages home:

I heard a fly buzz . . . , for example,
good scouts letting us know
what to expect, imaginary friends

modeled on people we once knew
gradually outnumbering those
still here in the flesh —

as in childhood games that began
with one person It, The Bear,
the rest of us children in the woods

until we were touched, one
by one, and *went over* —
the awful loneliness of being

the last child left, torn
between wanting to win
and wanting to be with the animals

who were at home in the dark,
whose eyes shone, who no longer answered
to the only names you knew them by.

WRAPPINGS

Gauze-draped islands
are lovely but redundant,
since language already upholsters
any world we live in, lumpy

under its covers after a million years
of revision, humans gathering
and regathering their wits.
Comforting florals, ruffles and flourishes,

austere geometrics. No right answer,
just one fabrication after another,
life in a spacious padded cell.
Each thought whisks by, and each emotion,

in crinolines, in corduroy. Batlike
we keep asking what's out there,
and never bump into the furniture
no matter how deftly we fly.

YOU ARE HERE

But the sign is over there,
its red arrow pointing
to X, one more letter

of the alphabet we use
to locate ourselves
in time and space —

there's plenty of room
for confusion, given the gap
between the map and the ground

we keep our feet on,
feeling our way,
listening for something

on the same wavelength,
for clues to our whereabouts
in words that come back to us

from the unknown, the ether
they've traveled through —
as if each syllable

were a question, a probe,
a toe in the water —
testing, testing — a tentative

caress, a lover's hand
asking the body to yield
its secrets, asking the world

to speak our language.

2

You are here: that's the news
you wake up to each morning,
and of course it's everything,

the crucial fact, the story
of your life, the words
that open your eyes —

as they did when you learned
to speak and to read,
when what had seemed to be nothing

turned out to be fog
and its lifting revealed
entire cities of possibilities:

busy intersections, dappled avenues,
redolent alleys no broom sweeps clean . . .
It all comes down to the body

and what it gives rise to:
the spirit that hovers above it,
released and held captive by language,

reciting an alphabet of longing.

THE AUTHOR

Flying Blind is Sharon Bryan's third collection of poems. The first two, *Salt Air* and *Objects of Affection,* were published by Wesleyan University Press. She is also the editor of *Where We Stand: Women Poets on Literary Tradition* (Norton, 1993). Her awards include an Academy of American Poets prize, the Discovery Award from *The Nation,* and two fellowships in poetry from the National Endowment for the Arts. She was poet-in-residence at The Frost Place in 1993. She teaches as a visiting writer, most recently at Dartmouth College and the University of Houston.